3 Day Guide to Milan

A 72-hour definitive guide on what to see, eat and enjoy in Milan, Italy

3 DAY CITY GUIDES

ISBN: 1512336033
ISBN-13: 978-1512336030

"The world is a book and he who doesn't travel only reads one page." – St. Augustine.

CONTENTS

1   Introduction to Milan   7

2   Milan Neighborhoods   25

3   How to Not Get Lost in Milan   29

4   Day 1 in Milan   32

5   Day 2 in Milan   40

6   Day 3 in Milan   48

7   Milan Local Cuisine   50

8   Best Places (Eat, Wine & Dine)   53

9   Milan Nightlife   58

10 Best Places to Stay (Luxurious, Mid-Range,   62
    Budget)

11 Other Interesting Places to Visit   67

12 Milan Travel Essentials   69

13 Italian Language Essentials   72

14 Milan Top Things to Do   77

    Conclusion   81

    More from This Author   83

1 INTRODUCTION TO MILAN

Santa Maria delle Grazie. Photo by <u>*Davide Oliva*</u>

Every Italian city conjures up a different image, as each one has a distinct character and a natural charm. Milan is just a typical city – traditional, classical, elegant, fashionable, historical, yet lively and very busy. On the surface, Milan displays a brash and tactless facade. This can be a deceiving charade as hidden beneath its cold and fearless coat, is a beauty emanating from a distinct character borne out of a rich past. It may only take a few hours before you can see and bask in the light of discovery, as it explicitly shines before you through the city's winding roads and alleys, its castles and churches, its museums and cathedrals.

Milan is proudly known as a fashion capital of the world, a designer's paradise serving as home to the iconic names of Valentino, Gucci, Versace, Prada, Armani, Dolce & Gabbana, and the who's who in the global fashion industry. Their grand creations and masterpieces grace their headquarters here – in this city of glamour and style.

Located on the northern side of Italy, serving as the capital of the region of Lombardy, this is a place where strokes of art are not just evidently presented in fashion, they can also be seen in its structures, with architecture that is detailed, unique and definitely impressive. The elegant composition of classicism, baroque and bourgeois designs are evident even on the exteriors of establishments. High, impressive buildings, palazzos and cathedrals dot the city and the grandest Gothic Cathedrals in the world can be found here.

Living in this city is almost 1.3 million hardworking, fashion conscious, business oriented populace who are always on the go. Thus, Milan is known to be the biggest industrial capital of Italy. This is also the reason why it may seem to be so lifeless on the outside but as soon as you uncover its core, Milan boasts a unique and lucid harmony of colors, aesthetic pride and legacy. The bright contrasts and remarkable contours make it a compelling, artsy niche for the creative minds of any medium.

Milan is snuggled up in the lower plains of the Padania, (a major plain in the Lombardy region of Italy) with several rivers surrounding the central city which block the first ice melts released by the alpines. Such a dramatic geographical and topographical landscape makes Milan unique in all aspects. This place with a land area of 181 sq.km and a sea-level rise of 122 meters, proved to be a very attractive and promising place which perhaps attracted the powerful might of the neighboring lands to conquer and take over Milan. The result has been a mixture of many influences, from all those who have ruled the land. The city of Milan now stands at the core of major industrial, political and commercial trade crisscrossing the major towns, cities and provinces of Italy. Unwind into a unique vacation as you step into one gorgeous city that will surely capture your imaginative soul.

History

The second largest and most populous city in Italy, Milan is the strategic capital of the region of Lombard. Historical records show that it was founded by the Insubres, Celtic people, in 6th century BC. The Insubres, as they were known at that time, built a village in the area that was later conquered by the Romans in 222 BC, getting the name "Mediolanum."

After 313 A.D., many churches were built and the

first bishop, St Ambrose, was appointed who later on became Milan's patron saint. In the succeeding years, the Roman Empire declined, and Milan became less necessary. The Lombards invaded the city in 539 A.D., which was followed by uncivilized invasions which destroyed the entire city. In the later years, Milan rose up from this repressive status and saw its rebirth in the 18th century, during the Carolingian years. It was a time of peace and systematic rule.

As the year 1000 arrived, Milan went through several political changes. Milan's archbishop became the most influential person and several years later, Milan went into expansion by conquering other cities within the area. Milan's government assumed democratic laws and it was during this time that they built Palazzo Della Ragione serving as the prime seat of government.

The 11th century saw more battles and conquests. The most predominant is the many attempts staged by Frederick of Swabia or Frederick Barbarossa to subjugate Milan until his defeat in 1176 which occurred in the eminent Battle of Legnano, or Battle of Royale, which has been used as the story behind the plot in a Giuseppe Verdi opera.

The year 1200 onwards heralded the onset of "feudalism" in Milan. This is the year marked with the aristocracy, from the affluent, modern and classy society, who were all eager to take Milan to the new century. Structural changes were made changing Milan's face, where old walls were extended around the city, new buildings were constructed and paved streets were developed.

The Visconti and Sforza Families

A legendary family name, the Viscontis, ruled two Italian noble dynasties (the first one in Pisa, which later on moved to Sardinia, and the other one in Milan). Ottone, the founder of Milan's Visconti regime, took over Milan in 1277. They became the "powers that be" which ruled the city for 170 years.

For many years, the Visconti era of Milan are marked with grandeur and prosperity, encompassing the surrounding areas and cities, who all acknowledged their supremacy. The last of the Visconti is Duke Filipe Maria, a royal lacking in good looks but has been known to be a great military leader and politician. He passed away in 1447 and the political direction of Milan took a turn towards republican rule. He was then succeeded by his daughter's husband, Francesco Sforza, in 1450, who took over the family's castle and political power. His rule was ensued by Milan's gaining of much sought-after peace after the many years of war against other nearby European countries like Venice and Florence.

Sforza was an instrument of positive change, in accordance with the innate characteristics of The Renaissance period, literally meaning "rebirth," an age of emergence and discovery. These characteristics matched the way Sforza family ruled Milan. Francesco's second son, Ludovico was the well-loved Sforza.

This Duke of Milan modernized the city by constructing many buildings and structures which included the famous historical structures of Castelo Sforzesco and the Ospedale Maggiore (now Ca' Granda). Castles and churches were also erected and the city became very influential, not just politically but economically as well. Ludovico gave importance to agricultural development as well and he also sought and called architects like Donato Bramante and Leonardo da Vinci to his court, thus making Milan inevitably the country's center for the culture and the arts. His rule was certainly one with a balance of power and might.

Spanish and Austrian Rule

The second half of the 17th century was marked by the renewal of Milan's religious and cultural life after a long time of uncertainty and the plague of 1630. From the 1500's to 1600's, these were the stagnant centuries when there were no developments, and most years are marked by oppression. Spanish and Austrians ruled the city and after much bloodshed, the unification of Italy began. In 1859, Austrians left the city, and two years later, the Kingdom of Italy was established which included Milan. This heralded the start of the modern-day Italy, and Milan was back in Italian hands. As Rome became the center of political affairs, Milan took the role as the country's economic and cultural capital.

In the early 1900s, Milan was at the helm of a rapid industrialization growth taking the lead over a young nation's economic, social and political debate. World War II, however, devastated the promising city which suffered under a harsh Nazi occupation. At that time, the city became the main center of the Italian resistance. The post-war years, however, brought forth the city into a prolonged economic boom, as large number of workers flowed from the Southern Italy. During the last decades, there has been a dramatic rise in the number of international immigrants.

Today, Milan is the main industrial, commercial and financial capital of Italy. A leading global city, its business district hosts Italy's main stock exchange and houses the headquarters of the largest national and international banks and companies. Known as the world's fashion and business capital, tourists are lured to Milan because of its rich history, and its dramatic structural landscape of museums, theatres and landmarks.

Climate

Milan has typical Mediterranean weather characterized by cold, foggy winters and sweltering, humid summers. The city of Milan is lucky to be covered by the mountains on the north shielding it from the worst of the Arctic chills, but there are still occasional drops in temperature with December as the coolest month. In summer, Milan can indeed be very, very hot as it is hit by heat waves, with July being the warmest month. Rain can come in intermittently any time within the year.

Spring

From March to May, weather in the city warms up rapidly after the winter freeze. Daytime highs reach up to 13°C (55°F) in March and 20°C (70°F) by May. Early spring nights can sometimes be cold. Rainfall in Milan is spread throughout the year and spring is not an exception.

Summer

Summer can be scorching with the temperature rising above 86°F (30°C) during August. The muggy heat can quickly reach a temperature high of 30°C. Coupled with thunderstorms and short, heavy bursts of rain, humidity in the city is sure to soar.

Autumn

September and October, after the scourging heat of summer is gone, are the popular months to visit Milan. Weather in fall is more comfortable with daytime highs of around 25°C (74°F) in September, falling to a cold 10°C (50°F) in November. It can also be wet at times, and fog is common throughout the autumn months.

Winter

Milan is at its dramatic best in winter. The charms of the city can also be enjoyed in December, January and February when the weather are slightly drier than most of the rest of the year, but the city is often overcast, foggy and bitingly cold. Daytime highs of 5°C (41°F) fall to -2°C (28°F) overnight, and snow falls occasionally.

Best Time to Visit

Any time of the year can be great to see the best the city can offer, but the summer months, especially July and August can be too hot for shopping and sightseeing. Spring and autumn are when the temperature is at its best (mildest) in Milan. For the trendy buffs and fashion enthusiasts, March and October are the months to be in town (when the major fashion collections are usually launched). Trade fairs and other fashion events are also held throughout the year. For football (soccer) fans, the season kicks off in September.

Language

Italian is the primary language (spoken and written) in Milan. In addition to this, a vast number of people in the metropolitan area speak the Milanese dialect, which they say is a Western variety of the Lombard language (romance language) which is closer to French, Romanish, and Occitan and to other Gallo-Italian languages. English is a moderately-spoken language here (primarily because of education and economic stature). A general portion of the populace are professionals who are friendly and helpful. But, it will be very useful to learn a bit of Italian to make it easier for you when communicating with the locals (Italian words are phonetically pronounced as they are, with emphasis oftentimes placed on the last syllable). A little understanding Latin also can be beneficial in helping you understand the inscriptions on ancient monuments and museums.

Helpful Tips

If your plane is landing or taking off from Malpensa airport, know in advance from which terminal it will do so. This will save you time and effort.

Smoking in public is generally prohibited in Milan (there are no-smoking symbols around the city). However, there are pubs and bars which allow their customers to smoke while drinking.

Tipping is quite flexible in Milan (cover/service charge is automatically added to your bill). You can give a token amount as a tip for the services, but you are not required to do so.

It is highly advisable to be always cautious and careful as the city is not free from bag snatchers and pickpockets (they sometimes operate on scooters). Do take care of your luggage and other personal belongings and beware of people offering free services. In the center of Milan, it is not unusual to be approached by people offering birdfeed or useless trinkets for free. Once you take whatever it is that they are giving, they will follow you asking for money.

Getting In

By Air

Milan has two main international airports, Linate and Malpensa, which serves as the gateways for major international airlines. It also has additional airports, Bergamo's Orio al Serio and Parma, which host budget airlines.

Malpensa is the main international airport with two terminals connected by a free shuttle bus service. Be warned though that these shuttles are very small thus long queues tend to form and passengers may need to wait for quite some time for the transfers. This airport is connected directly to Milan via a railway link, the Malpensa Express Train system. Buses and taxis are also available which can take you directly to the city, but riding a taxi can be quite expensive. The only taxis which charges a fixed rate are those registered in Milan. Taxis from outlying cities can still take you to Milan but will charge you higher. One sign to look out for will be a card in the window or rear of the driver/passenger seats, a sure clue that you are riding in a non-Milanese taxi. You can request the fixed fee but if the driver refuses, then take the next taxi in the rank.

Linate Airport is smaller than Malpensa but has an efficient one runway setup and is very close to the city center. It is serviced by airlines flying to domestic and to other European destinations. This airport is situated close to the city and is accessible by buses of the city public transport network. There is even a dedicated bus service, called "Starfly", which can bring passengers from Linate airport, en route to Lambrate Railways station, finally arriving at the Milan central station.

Taxis from Linate to the city center cost around €12-20 depending on traffic conditions. The minimum charge is €12. If you are going to the center, ignore all the guys standing at the exit to the terminal saying "taxi!" They are for destinations outside central Milan (i.e., outlying cities) and will charge a minimum of €70. Queues for regular taxis can get long during peak commute hours (early evening) and are particularly bad during Fashion Week.

By Train

If you are coming in from other European cities via train, the main railway station is the Central Station (Milano Centrale) which is served by Trenitalia, the State Railways. Regular express and fast trains serve all Italian cities (Turin, Venice, Rome, Naples, Florence and many others), and some European cities (Barcelona, Zurich, Geneva, Munich, Paris, Stuttgart, Zagreb, Vienna, etc.). The station building is in itself worth a visit being a masterpiece of rationalist architecture.

Getting Around

Milano Streetview. Photo by <u>*Bert Kaufmann*</u>

Milan's city center is quite compact and can easily be explored via several options. Public transportation has an excellent network that comes in three modes traversing throughout the city and the suburbs as well. The primary public transportation network system is run by Azienda Trasporti Milanesi (ATM) which operates most major carriers (underground lines, trams and buses). Just look for the ATM sign to know your options.

For prices or transport fares, there is a single ticket journey that may cost less but there is a time limit for that. Travel time, which includes transfers and changes of buses or tram lines, needs to be done within 90 minutes for one ticket that costs €1.50.

You can change Metro lines on one ticket, too, but as soon as you leave a Metro station you can't use the same ticket on the Metro again – each ticket can only include one Metro trip.

There are also tickets and passes for multi-day trips. Just make sure to have the ticket validated before each use. Always keep those tickets handy and be ready to show them to the inspectors at the trains, buses and trams.

For more information on ATM ticket fares and types, please visit: http://www.atm-mi.it/en/ViaggiaConNoi/Biglietti/Pages/Tipologie.aspx

Metro

Milan's subway system is fairly easy to use. It has three key lines that stop at major tourist spots (red, green & yellow). It is also easy to identify as it has a big white M (against a red background) serving as its logo. The lines are color coded: MM1, red (rossa); MM2, green (verde); MM3, yellow (gialla); MM5, violet (lilla). Line MM4 is under construction. The subway network lines split into different sections and its 103 stations cover most areas of town. Trains run every 1-3 min, 06:00-23:59 (02:00 on Saturday nights).

As with any central station, precautionary measures should be taken in order to ensure safety. Be careful as there are groups of pickpockets around the metro ticket vending machines at the main station

(Centrale). You also have the option to purchase your tickets in advance or buy them at the ticket office.

Tram

Ride in a tram in Milan and experience a unique way of exploring the city. The ride itself will be an adventure on its own. You can find trams almost everywhere in the city, running on rail lines (above-ground) traversing through the streets of Milan. They provide a perfect way to savor the view of what you're passing through. These trams are indeed a source of fun and enjoyment as well.

These exciting pieces of operational transportation include modern and traditional tram lines which are very similar to those found in the streets of San Francisco, which are antique carriages with wooden paneling and glass chandeliers. There is also a restaurant tram and a party tram with disco music. Milan also has significant historical trams which showcase the city's rich cultural and historical heritage, on board the "serie 1500" type, dating back as early as 1929. Hop on this moving museum on the road and marvel at the experience.

Many tram stops have electronic information panels which announce the waiting time for passengers.

Bus

The most convenient form of transportation, as

with many other cities, will be the ever dependable, comfortable buses. It may take consume more travel time depending on your destination but it is still a very much reliable mode of transportation with many available routes. The operation time, however, varies, and some lines do close early. Just make sure to verify and double check the routes, especially for night traveling. There are also bus lines that connect Milan to other cities nearby. There's an inter-urban ticket that you can purchase giving you the option to travel within Milan or outside of the city. Simply inquire at the ATM ticket booths.

Radio Bus

If your itinerary is constricted to several places within an exact period of time, you may opt to take the Radio Bus. These are special shuttle services that will stop at dedicated places. Just make sure to mentally note and remember the pick-up locations so as not to lose your way. There are also silent rules here like ladies are given priorities as a form of courtesy. Tickets may cost €2 and you can make advance purchases or just pay when you get on the bus.

Train

As in any other European city, one of the primary modes of transportation in Milan is the train. The Suburban Railway System or most commonly known as the S-lines run every 6-15 minutes and traverses through many stations in the city and the surrounding areas. The city trains though run less frequently than Metro trains. Lines are identified with the "S" added with a number like S1, S2 and are inter-connected to each other.

Taxi

You can hail a taxi from any designated taxi stand within the city but be warned as they may be expensive. Phone bookings are also available, just dial 848.814.781 and a taxi will just come to pick you up at the nearest taxi stand. In such cases, you will be charged from the time that the driver answered the call. Rates are higher in the evening as they charge extra for night trips.

By Bike

Be fit and fab as you pedal your way around Milan by bike. There are bicycles for rent or you may arrange your bike rentals online (BikeDistrict is one website you can go to register). Once registered, you will be given suggested itineraries as well as maps of the bike routes and the schedule of cycling-related events and services.

On Foot

Exploring the city on foot is another possibility. Take a pleasant and leisurely walk from one tourist spot to another (most are just a short distance from each other). Several streets are only open to pedestrians so you can take all the time you need.

Some people say that the best way to get to know a place and its people is to be there, in the streets, trying to discover the stories neatly hidden in its every turn. See the pathways and structures and marvel at the sight of elegantly dressed and fashionable garbed people walking in the streets of Milan. Savor a cup of cappuccino as you watch how Milanese life goes by. Just make sure that you have a map handy to know exactly where you are heading.

2 MILAN'S KEY NEIGHBORHOODS

Milan is the largest industrial town of Italy with a population of about 1.3 million people. The city houses many beautiful ancient buildings, monuments and churches. Italy's second largest city, Milan, is divided into vibrant districts full of nightlife, stunning architecture and museums. Here a few of the key districts to place on your itinerary.

Brera

Situated in Old Milan, Brera is an artistic neighborhood well known for its bohemian vibe. And why not? For it is here where you will find the Brera Art Gallery as well as the Brera Academy of fine Arts located within the beautiful Palazzo Brera. Head to this district to peruse antiques offerings, art galleries, old churches, vibrant street markets and trendy bars. A metro ride to the Lanza stop (green line) will place you in the Brera district.

Monte Napoleone

Dubbed Montenapo by the locals, this chic district is where you will find the *Quadrilatero della moda* which features the top Italian fashion designers, inclusive of their high end jewelry and ready-to-wear collections. Whether you're after Armani, Versace or a little Dolce & Gabbana, via Monte Napoleone is where you will come to get it. Art lovers will also find the Museo Bagatti Valsecchi and the Museo Poldi Pezzoli within this district. Take the metro (yellow line) to stop Monte Napoleone.

Corso Magenta

Corso Magenta is an important and popular district in Milan. It is within this district where you will view cultural sites such as the Teatro Lotta and Leonardo Da Vinci's Last Supper in the church of Santa Maria delle Grazie. In addition to its stunning architecture, Corso Magenta is also another popular shopping street within Milan along with nearby Corso Vercelli. To reach this district take the metro (red line) to stop Cadorna F.n. and walk down via Carducci to Corso Magenta.

La Scala & Duomo

These two districts are readily accessible from the same metro stop (red or yellow line) –Duomo. Head north to visit the district of La Scala which is aptly named for the world renowned opera house that you will find here, *Teatro alla Scala*. You can delve into the history of this gem with a visit to the adjacent Museo Teatrale alla Scala. Other treasures within this district include the Galleria Vittorio

Emanuele and the church of San Giuseppe.

A few steps south will put you in the heart of the Duomo district –Piazza Duomo. It is here where visitors from around the world come to view Milan's most important cathedral, the Duomo. Other key stops within the Piazza and the surrounding area include Galleria Vittorio Emanuele II, Palazzo Reale and the Renaissance church of Santa Maria presso San Satiro.

Giardini

Located in the north eastern part of Milan, Giardini hosts beautiful green spaces that invite you to take a calming stroll. This refuge can be reached by taking the metro (red line) to stop Palestro and while you are there, take a look inside Milan's Museum of Natural Science or the nearby Villa Reale which houses the Galleria d'Arte Moderna (Gallery of Modern Art).

Ticinese

This working class district was the former home of Milan's port and is where you can venture to see the picturesque waterways of the Navigli. It's a lively area full of small shops, cafes and restaurants that make the visit well worth it. In addition, you will also find the church of San Lorenzo as well as the church of Sant'Eustorgio. To journey here, take the metro (green line) to stop Sant'Agostino.

Castello & Triennale

These adjacent districts located in the north western neighborhood of Milan have much to offer visitors who favor history coupled with a side trip through an expansive green. Triennale is known for its beautiful Sempione Park where within its green space you can find the Palazzo dell'Arte along with the Triumphal Arc. To reach Trinanale take the metro (red line) to Cordorna FN. The nearby Castello district, reachable by metro (red line) stop Cairoli, features the Sforza Castle and within its museum is Michelangelo's Rondanini Pietà.

3 HOW NOT TO GET LOST IN MILAN

Milan, Italy. Photo by Jess Wood

Getting lost in a foreign city is something that happens to most of us at some point during our travels. Whether they admit it or not, even the most seasoned of travelers can get confused at times. Milan is one of the cities in Italy where you can easily get lost, as it's not a place you will master in one day. What do you do when you discover you have no idea of where you are?

If you get lost, take advantage of popular landmarks in Milan and use them as reference points. Most free city maps include landmark locations, allowing you to quickly reroute yourself should you be in the vicinity of one of them.

For example, the **Duomo Cathedral** is the most popular central landmark in the city and serves as a useful reference point. The famous opera house **La Scala**, is another popular central landmark that can help you get back on track. **Corso Buenos Aires** is the largest shopping street in Milan and connects the city center to the northern part of Milan. The ever visible **Velasca Tower** is a mushroom-shaped building located in Milan's southern Università district.

There are also many sacred sites and religious buildings that can be used as a point of location when you get lost in Milan. By taking note of your surroundings, you not only help yourself but you also make it easier for others to assist you as well.

Thankfully, there are also a number of **tourist info centers** in Milan. In addition to maps you can receive information on shopping malls, lakes, restaurants, hotels and so forth. Most tourist info centers are open from Monday to Friday – 9:00 AM to 6:00 PM, with closures during the national holidays. Two prominent tourist info centers can be found in **Galleria Vittorio Emanuele II** (near the Piazza della Scala end) and the **IAT Central Station** (located near platform 21).

Another option is to ask the locals. Some tourists are uncomfortable with this idea due to language barriers, however you will find that many Milanese speak some English and will be more than happy to help you.

Lastly, if you are completely lost and have nowhere to turn, grab a cab and provide your hotel address and contact information. As a general rule, only take the recommended official taxis (painted in white and yellow).

Getting lost in a big city like Milan can be a fun experience; you will uncover new things you wouldn't have which is one of the hidden joys of travel.

4 MILAN DAY 1

Step back in time and enjoy a great Milanese breakfast of cappuccino and brioches as you savor an early morning breeze at a very historic 19th-century Milanese eatery, Pasticceria Marchesi. Known across the city for its delicious pastries, chocolate and panettone, it is located right at the entrance of Corso Magenta, at the corner of Via Santa Maria alla Porta. This famous and well-loved pastry shop was able to retain its original interiors and ambience. Just sit there, relax and feel the Milanese beat before you start exploring the city.

Via Santa Maria alla Porta, 11a

Phone: +39 02 862 770

Duomo di Milano (Milan Cathedral)

No Milanese trip will be complete without seeing the most important structure in this city. An exceptionally large and elaborate Gothic cathedral proudly standing in the heart of Milan, on the main square and is called the Duomo di Milano. All the streets of the city somehow lead to this Cathedral because of its central location. Its facade is very impressive causing you to wonder how it came into being. This is one of the most famous buildings in Europe and the second largest cathedral in the world.

Duomo di Milano. Photo by Bryce Edwards

It was actually constructed in 1385 by the then Bishop Antonio da Saluzzo, supported by Duke Visconti. Together, they embarked on an ambitious dream of creating the world's biggest church. Construction dragged on for centuries (spanning nearly six) and construction finally commenced in 1965. Occupying the most important site in the ancient Roman city of Mediolanum, this Gothic cathedral has been a mixture of different styles and inspirations bringing forth a magnificent and impressive architectural piece. This is considered to be the most representative monuments of the city and stands as an iconic symbol of Milan.

The building's exterior is made of brick faced with white marble providing a very eccentric and egotistical design. It has five naves or ships, standing mighty and proud in its facade. Stained glass windows adorn and shade the interiors while the roof has pinnacles and spines topped with statues that overlook the city of Milan. Guests can walk on the roof and can have an up close view of the detailed designs and architecture of the cathedral. Up there, you will be surrounded by more than 4000 marble figures, each one is reputedly a unique piece. It has a total of 3,400 statues perched atop the cathedral and at its highest point is the Madonnina, a golden statue of the Virgin Mary which shines whenever the light strikes the image.

Piazza del Duomo

Phone: +39 02 7202 2656

Castello Sforzesco

Get a glimpse of one of the most colorful era in Milan's historical past. Set foot in a four-walled fortress, with a square tower at each corner. This castle served as home to noble and aristocratic families of Milan's bygone eras. It will be like traces of a majestic history unfolding before your very eyes. The Viscontis of the 1300's and the Sforzas of the 1400's, all resided in this place. The Sforzesco Castle stood as witness to the fierce rivalries between families in Renaissance Italy. This structure actually became a showcase of power and prestige. Today, it houses various art collections from Paleolithic age to the recent decades, all carefully preserved in 12 mini-museums and archives. It is now the home of prestigious art collections such as the Pietà Rondanini, Michelangelo's final masterpiece.

Many of Milan's city dwellers have mixed feelings towards this structure. Somehow, it reminds them of the many years when foreign conquerors ruled over their land. It was only during the recent years that this was somehow changed as the castle took a new role as a comforting cultural place.

Piazza Castello, 27029

Phone: +39 02 8846 3700

Sempione Park

Walk along the greens of Parco Sempione, rest for a while and let your thoughts wander in this large park located near the Sforzesco Castle. This place used to be a hunting ground of the Visconti in the 14th century and today, it has changed to become a charming park which has a number of noteworthy buildings and monuments, all with historical stories and legacy, including the historic triumphal arc, which served as a silent witness to Napoleon's downfall in 1815. A forty-seven hectare large park nicely laid out in a landscape style with winding paths, grassy areas, tall trees and a picturesque bridge across a central pond. Many events are held in this park for the months of spring and summer.

Parco Sempione, Milan. Photo by <u>Mike and Annabel Beales</u> CCBY-ND

Piazza Sempione, 20154

Phone: +39 02 8846 7383

Pinacoteca of Brera

Marvel at Milan's grand art collection – an impressive collection of rare masterpieces in one of Italy's most precious art galleries. Thanks to Napoleon, who confiscated much of Italy's best pieces of art during the 18th century and deposited them in Milan, the Pinacoteca di Brera is a world-class museum with an astonishing assortment of fine paintings. This gallery is housed inside Palazzo di Brera and has more than 40 rooms. Works by Italian painters like Raphael, Tintoretto, Veronese and Caravaggio are featured in the collection. European masters like Rembrandt, van Dyck and Goya are well represented as well.

The Palazzo used to be a convent following a religious order called "Humiliati" in the 14th century. The Jesuits took over the place and converted it into a school, a convent, a library and an astronomical observatory at the site in the 17th century. It was during that time that they started building the Palazzo which was completed almost two hundred years later. The design was initially done in Baroque style but was remodeled in neoclassical architecture by the end of the 18th century, from the order of the empress Maria Teresa d'Austria.

This two-story structure is marked by stone columns, pillars and portals. It also has an inner courtyard where you can find the big bronze statue of Napoleon dressed as Mars the peacemaker. This Gallery is entirely different from any other gallery in Italy as it boasts of a collection that did not start as a private collection but rather, it emanated from a political will, born from a state collection. These works of art were items and valuable pieces confiscated by Napoleon from the convents and churches from all over Italy in the 18t century.

Today, you can view and admire these pieces inside the Brera National Art Gallery where they are displayed chronologically.

Via Brera, 28, 20121

+39 02 7226 3264

Tickets: 10 €, reduced ticket 7,50 €

La Scala Theatre

Teatro alla Scala. Photo by David Davies

Allow this cultural and historical experience to take your art indulgence from canvas to the stage. There's no other way to cap your first day in Milan than to watch and enjoy a classical performance at the premier and the best opera house in the world! This theatre has a magnanimous reputation as a distinguished venue.

It has showcased rare talents and brilliant

performances since its first performance in 1778. It was built by the Empress Maria Theresa of Austria, at that time that their family ruled over Milan. Just like the other structures built during those times, La Scala Opera House follows a neoclassical style of architecture using predominantly red-and-gold colors. This theatre is also known for its superb acoustics, which befits the saying, "once heard and experienced, it will be something that you will never forget".

Via Filodrammatici, 2, 20121

Phone: +39 02 88791

5 MILAN DAY 2

After an exhilarating first day in Milan, anyone should deserve to have a heavenly breakfast at Parma & Co. It's the Milanese temple of prosciutto di Parma and gnocco fritto, so enjoy it here as well as the other regional delicacies from Emilia Romagna – but brunch here is the best! Savor their tasty lasagna, meatballs, then cap your meal with their delectable handmade crostata.

Via Delio Tessa, 2, 20121 Milano, Italy
Tel: +39 02 8909 6720

Santa Maria delle Grazie - "The last supper" by Leonardo da Vinci in Milan

Set foot in this church and convent and see for yourself one of the greatest art masterpieces of all times. This architectural complex was built in 1463 for the Dominicans. The structure has a drum-shaped dome, with large semi-circular apses and is surrounded by columns, cloister and refectory. This is one of the architectural feats done during the Renaissance period but the most important aspect of this church and convent lies on its northern wall.

This is where Leonardo da Vinci wielded his strokes with brushes, creating a shining symbol of creative grandeur.

Santa maria delle grazie Milano. Photo by Francesco Sgroi

The mural painting depicted the "Last Supper" and was completed using watercolors combining light and strong perspectives in 1487. The great artist depicted the scene focusing on the different reactions of the 12 apostles after Christ said, "One of you will betray me". Each reaction was brilliantly captured showing the impact of Christ's word to the apostles. Considered to be an ambiguous work of art, it is open to many interpretations, yet the distinct quality and inspiration will always stand out. You will find the "Last Supper" in the dining hall of Santa Maria Delle Grazie.

This work has been recently rediscovered but, unfortunately, it was not done in oil but in tempera on a two-layered surface of plaster which was not damp-proof. This technique decreases the chance for preservation and it is said that sooner or later, the enormous painting will disappear because of the dampness. A lot of effort and actual work has been put into the restoration of it, and the last one, which was in 1999, gave the work its original colors and removed the paint of the older restorations. The painting is maintained under specific conditions and visitors are only allowed to visit for a short time. Catching a glimpse of this mural during your visit to Milan is well worth it.

Piazza di Santa Maria delle Grazie, 20123

Phone: +39 02 467 6111

Tickets: 6,50 €, reduced tickets 3,25 €

The Galleria Vittorio Emanuele II

Be enthralled by the famous Galleria Vittorio Emanuele II or most commonly known now as "The Galleria." Shop in a connected alley, glass-vaulted arcades, connecting the two of the most important landmarks of Milan, the Duomo and the La Scala (there are entrances from each one).

Here you can see arches overlapping each other, supported by columns or piers. The effect is truly amazing. At the center is a dome in octagonal shape, reaching a height of 47 meters. You will notice that in each shop inside this place bears a uniformed insignia of gold letters on a black background. You can also see the amazing mosaics on the floor. The Galleria is named after the first King of the Kingdom of Italy. It was built in the first half of 19th century by Giuseppe Mengoni.

Today, this place offers a different and classy way of shopping in a four-story architectural feat. The Galleria is full of elegant shops where you can buy an assortment of things from clothes and jewelry to books and paintings.

Shopping in Milan. Photo by Mike and Annabel Beales *CC BY-ND*

There are also bars and restaurants which may cater to your dining needs. Christmas is another treat as they deck the halls with decor, the most prominent being the beautiful Christmas tree adorned with Swarovski crystals.

Piazza Duomo, 20123

Phone: +39 02 7740 4343

Basilica di Sant'Ambrogio

Basilica di Sant Ambrogio, Aisle, Milan. Photo by Allan Parsons

Do not miss Milan's second most important cathedral, the Basilica di Sant' Ambrogio. This medieval church was rebuilt in the 11th century following the Romanesque style of architecture. It has an elegant courtyard and the entire cathedral has remarkable details. The exterior boasts a central large atrium with two towers of different heights.

The interiors are equally impressive with pillars, a 4th century sarcophagus carved with biblical scenes, a 9th century silver altar, and a canopy hanging over it dating back to the 10th century. One noticeable piece is a 10th-century bronze serpent called the "Serpent Column" located on the right side of the nave, placed atop a short column.

This basilica was named after its founder, the 4th-century bishop of Milan and the city's patron Saint Ambrose, whose remains are still housed in the church, displayed in a crypt built in the 10th century. A small chapel off the right aisle of the nave known as the Sacello di San Vittore in Ciel d'Oro features 5th-century mosaics.

Piazza Sant' Ambrogio, 15, 20123

Phone: +39 02 8645 0895

The Navigli

Walk along the most charming district in Milan, the Navigli. Catch the sunset and heave a sigh of awe and admiration as the rays slowly reflects on the waters of Navigli's canals.

Its history traces back to the 12th century with the first canal, Ticinello, being opened in 1179. This canal made possible the building of the Major Naviglio (Naviglio Grande). Important engineers worked towards the realization of these canals that includes the genial sluice gate conceived by Leonardo da Vinci after Ludovico il Moro commissioned him for the project at the end of the 15th century. In 1980, an improvement project of the area began.

Today, visitors to Milan can enjoy a 55-minute

cruise along the remaining Navigli Lombardi. Tour boats depart from the point where Darsena, the city's historic port, and the Naviglio Grande, Milan's most famous canal, meet. Strolling along the narrow paths is a popular way to explore the Navigli neighborhood too.

Navigli. Photo by Massimiliano Calamelli

The Navigli at one point in time became very popular as a place for street markets and shops. Nowadays, this place is famous as a base for Milan's nightlife scene. A lot of people come here to wine and dine and it had transformed into a very fashionable area serving as a meeting point for models, artists, university students, most of whom spend their nights hopping from one bar to another. But behind all these concepts, Navigli was able to retain its inherent charm with a natural, unassuming atmosphere. Here, you can still find traditional workshops, the simple cafes, and the colorful courtyards. Everywhere you look, there's something beautiful to see.

6 MILAN DAY 3

Lake Como. Photo by <u>George Dement</u>

The best is yet to come for this trip in Milan. But first, one should get some energy-packed meal at Unico - a unique restaurant that will give you a breath-taking view of the city while having your brunch. Unico offers wonderful food choices, following a different theme each weekend (based on regional foods such as gnocchi brunch or Liguria brunch). The place will be a best spot to relish the experience of the last two days spent in the city. It is more expensive than the average, but definitely worth it.

Viale Achille Papa, 30, 20149 Milano, Italy
Tel: +39 02 3921 4847

Lake Como

It's time sail along the scenic Lake Como, one of the most spectacular lakes of Italy. This place is just an hour travel from the city, yet it is packed with heaps of surprises. Lake Como is one experience which cannot be missed as this lake is acclaimed as a natural jewel near Milan. A feast for a weary soul, here is where you will enjoy your third day in Milan. Savor the view of the glassy waters with picturesque mountains in the background and the not so distant Alps further behind. Here, everything seems surreal.

The lake and its villages can be explored on foot (at times, you may need to take the bus). Enjoy the breathtaking vista before you as you take some time for a leisurely lunch, and then grab the chance to stroll around the town itself. Within the villages you will find top-notch shopping, set against a dramatic backdrop of the Italian homes of Hollywood celebrities, such as George Clooney. It goes without saying that this can be a one-of-a-kind experience you will treasure forever.

7 MILAN LOCAL CUISINE

Although Milan is a city that changes its mind as quickly as fashion trends come and go, it remains one of the strongest bastions of traditional Italian cooking, where homemade elements are still very much praised and appreciated. There are trattorias, enoteche (wine bars) and restaurants everywhere that offer traditional Milanese and Italian dishes to eat.

Dining times tend to be a shade earlier than in Rome or Florence, with lunch generally served between 12:30PM and 2:30PM and dinner from 7:30PM to 9:30PM. Dinner, and sometimes lunch, are usually preceded by the great Milanese institution, the aperitivo—a glass of sparkling wine or a Campari soda. As far as the most popular Italian cuisine in Milan goes, here are a few traditional dishes to consider when touring the city.

Cotoletta alla Milanese

This signature Milanese dish is comprised of a tender veal chop coated with breadcrumbs and then pan fried to a warm golden brown. This dish is most commonly accompanied by fresh lemon wedges but go for a gentle squeeze if you prefer your breadcrumb coating crisp.

La Barbajada

Reportedly named after the waiter who invented it, Neapolitan Domenico Barbajada, this delicious beverage is a frothy combination of cream, chocolate and coffee. Enjoy it cold in the summer or warm in the winter.

Panettone

Panettone is a light yeast cake that contains ingredients such as ingredients such as flour, eggs, water, dried candied and butter. Panettone originated in Milan and is now a traditional dessert enjoyed throughout Italy, especially during the Christmas season.

Risotto alla Milanese

Risotto all Milanese is a rich and creamy Milanese dish of rice, white wine, onion, saffron, bone marrow and grated Parmesan cheese. The saffron gives this dish the golden tint that has made it famous the world over.

Cooking classes in Milan

Hungry for a little more? Why not learn the passion behind the food by taking a cooking class in Milan? There are few souvenirs greater than learning to cook the local cuisine and here are a few cooking classes that suit the needs and budget of everyone.

Cook in Milano

http://www.cookinmilano.com/

La Scuola de la Cucina Italiana

http://www.lacucinaitaliana.it/default.aspx?idPage=1406

Teatro7

http://www.teatro7.com/ (click link in upper right of page for English)

8 BEST PLACES (EAT, WINE & DINE)

Bruschetta. Photo by _Prawee Nonthapun_

Sitting down for a Milanese meal can be quite ergonomically satisfying and very fulfilling. Veering away from the norm of pasta, Milanese cuisine consists more so of rice. The main ingredient of their dishes is butter and it can be found and tasted as part of any delectable delight and masterpiece. You can catch a hint of it in your "risotto", in your veal cutlets and in the famous "panettone".

Do not forget to sample the famous "risotto alla

milanese," a special rice dish made with saffron.
Another must try savory dish is the "busecca" or
"busecconi," a dish made of stewed tripe. Italian
meals come in four courses (some may find this too
heavy, but that is actually the way that they enjoy
their meals). A famous choice for second courses is
the Cotoletta alla Milanese are breaded veal meat,
with or without bone and fried in butter (health
conscious uses olive oil). If you prefer sweet dishes,
Milan has two of the most known Italian cakes: the
panettone, which is traditionally made for
Christmas, and the "colomba", which is made for
Easter. Milan is also known for its exquisite cheese
products like stracchino, mascarpone, grana of Lodi
and the tasty gorgonzola. And, of course, do not
miss grabbing a bite of the truly delectable and
world-famous salame Milano, a salami with a very
fine grain, yet has a distinct flavor and taste.

Milan boasts a long list of world-class restaurants
and cafés, characterized by innovative cuisine and
design. The following are just some of the suggested
places where you can wine and dine:

Il Luogo Di Aimo e Nadia

A family restaurant, run by Aimo and Nadia,
offering traditional Tuscan cuisine. This restaurant
has been recently awarded two Michelin stars. They
serve subtle Italian flavored dishes such as "fantasy
of Tuscan suckling pig with apple compote,"
"chestnut flour cake" and "raw tartar of wild hare
with red chicory and celeriac." The restaurant walls

are covered with bold abstract artworks. Service in this place is impeccable.

Via Privata Raimondo Montecuccoli, 6

Phone: +39 024 168 86

Giacomo

A Milanese institution opened by Giacomo Bulleri in 1958. This is where high fashion and local business meet in an obscure location just 15 minutes from the historical center. Dine with Milan's elegant locals and savor Giacomo's specialty – seafood (uber-fresh) prepared with wonderful Italian simplicity. Try their linguine too, with scampi and zucchini flowers. Decor in this place is something to be marveled at as well, with its celadon colored walls, bookshelves and a striking mosaic floor.

Da Giacomo, Via Pasquale Sottocorno 6

Phone: +39 02 76 02 33 13

Ceresio 7

Discover this new kid on the block in dining experiences. Recently inaugurated, this bar, restaurant and swimming pool, owned by Dan and Dean Caten of Dsquared[2] is perched on the rooftop of the label's design headquarters. Decor is a throwback to the 1930's. Food is traditional Italian using the finest ingredients from a hearty yet innovative menu from renowned chef Elio Sironi. It will be best to call in advance to ensure seats.

Ceresio 7, Via Ceresio 7

+39 02 31 03 92 21

Pizzeria Spontini

Their tagline, "Simply Perfecto", says it all! Renowned as the one of the best pizzerias in town, this place opened in the 1950's and was able to retain its original well-loved recipe from way, way back. Please be reminded that they only serve one pizza flavor – margherita pizza. This melt in your mouth pizza has thick, yet crispy base topped with tomato, mozzarella, oregano and anchovies. Classic and definitely unforgettable.

Erba Brusca

Located on the edge of the city, on the Navigli, is this restaurant serving creative Mediterranean cuisine. It is best described as a "vegetable garden with a kitchen" where guests can enjoy their meals in an outdoor, garden setting where mixed herbs and seasonal veggies are grown. In this resto, the focus is on natural, local, organic produce. The must try list includes couscous with smoked mackerel and yoghurt sauce, savory tarte tatin made with seasonal vegetables and spaghetti with clams, fish eggs and fresh herbs.

Strada Alzaia Naviglio Pavese, 286

Phone: +39 02 8738 0711

9 MILAN NIGHTLIFE

Nightclub. Photo by Bruce Turner

Milan offers a lively, active and highly entertaining nightlife. It starts early and ends up late which is just perfect for those who want to have a full night out.

Choose from the two main areas of entertainment in Milan, as these places have the highest concentration of bars, lounges and nightspots. These are Brera Gallery and Navigli Canal. Please take note that nightclubs in Milan are known for playing a wide repertoire and genre of music, from jazz to rock. In Garibaldi, you may find spots which are frequented by models and stars. During summer, the nightlife moves in the direction of the Idroscalo, where houses other popular discos. For those who would rather spend a calm evening, having an aperitif or a cocktail, there is the Navigli and Via Tortona. Just do remember that Milan is not free from traffic, even at night, so it will be very advisable to leave early and take either the tram, the metro or the bus to get there without much hassle. Here are few of the suggested places where you can unwind:

Le Trottoir

A great place to just sit down, relax while you savor a few drinks. Here you will find a great happy hour along with live music and their impressive buffet includes pasta, focaccia, risotto, couscous, vegetables and more.

Piazza XXIV Maggio, 1

Phone: +39 02 837 8166

Rolling Stone

This lively nightspot is a discotheque and plays live rock music. It also features Top DJ's from all around Milan. You may want to check out the schedule of their live performances by calling the number listed below. This venue is known for their impressive line-up of acts.

C.so XXII Marzo, 32 – 20135

Phone: +39 02 733 172

Bar Magenta

This locale offers sandwiches, snacks and beers which can be enjoyed amidst a classic art deco interiors.

Via Carducci 13

Phone: +39 02 805 3808

Nottingham Forest

A place with a unique character all its own. Merging furniture and props from the Far East, the Caribbean and Africa to create a signature global style. Cocktail enthusiasts gather beneath suspended objects and between original pieces of "memories," souvenirs from travels to distant countries. The international influences continue with the magical drinks.

Viale Piave, 1, 20129

Phone: +39 02 789311

Le Barrique Wine Bar

A sophisticated little spot – a bar, wine shop and restaurant in one. The interior has wooden floors, a large classic bar, bare brick walls and arches on the ceiling. Bottles of wine are everywhere, along with more curious decor like metallic ties and artist prints. A good place to have a cozy night out with friends.

Via Anfiteatro, 12

Phone: +39 02 8050 9260

10 BEST PLACES TO STAY (LUXURIOUS, MID-RANGE, BUDGET)

Park Hyatt Milan. Photo by Brian Johnson & Dane Kantner

Luxurious

Armani Hotel Milano

Following the trend of world-class luxury, this is the second Armani hotel to be recently launched after the Armani hotel in Burj Khalifa, Dubai. The Milan hotel also has austere and powerful exterior. The same trademark was followed creating a world of harmony and privacy, with uncompromising attention to luxury, calm and beauty.

The Armani style and philosophy defines every detail of the 95 guestrooms and suites of Armani Hotel Milano. Each element has been personally designed by Giorgio Armani and has been chosen for its sculptural, aesthetic and sensual qualities.

Via Manzoni 31, 20121

Phone: +39 02 8883 8888

Four Seasons Milan

A classic, luxurious accommodation in a dramatically reborn 15th-century convent. A host of delightful features from the past remain, including 15th century Renaissance cloisters and frescoes, and an 18th-century impressive fireplace and superb neo-classical facade. Four Seasons Hotel Milan offers 118 spacious guest rooms and 51 suites surrounding a peaceful, landscaped courtyard. The Hotel's guest rooms blend historic architectural details with contemporary Italian design.

Via Gesu, 6/8, 20121

Phone: +39 02 77088

Park Hyatt Milan

An elegant boutique hotel, set in a palatial classical building dating back to 1870. The hotel features exclusive interiors designed by Ed Tuttle. The hotel is home to restaurants VUN and La Cupola, treasured for their refined atmosphere and gourmet cuisine. This hotel also has The Spa, offering an oasis of pure relaxation and rejuvenation, with clean lines and mellow lighting, travertine and a pastel Venetian stucco finish showcasing elegance and professionalism while providing an escape from the hectic outside world.

Via Tommaso Grossi, 1

Phone: +39 02 8821 1234

Mid-range

Antares Hotel Reubens

This family oriented hotel is located close to the city center. It has well-appointed rooms and world-class facilities and amenities. In addition to its own restaurant, it also has a fitness center, a bar lounge and a coffee shop. A complimentary buffet breakfast is served daily.

Via Pietro Paolo Rubens, 21, 20148

Phone: +39 02 40302

Hotel Monopole

A comfortable 3-star hotel which is very near the Central Station. This hotel offers an internet point, free wi-fi Internet connection and easy access to the bus terminal for Linate, Malpensa and Bergamo Orio al Serio airports. Recently renovated, this hotel offers numerous services. All the rooms are comfortable and modern and are equipped with a safe, satellite TV and free wi-fi.

Via Fabio Filzi, 43, 20124

Phone: +39 02 6698 4972

Budget

Lancaster Hotel

This is one charming hotel that offers excellent yet affordable accommodation. They also offer great service and an optimal location. Rooms are reasonably priced and the hotel is in a very quiet location, close to delightful restaurants.

Via Abbondio Sangiorgio, 16, 20145

Phone: +39 02 344705

Hotel Panizza

A fine hotel located near the train stations. Rates

are affordable with well-appointed rooms, great service from a very friendly staff. Nice shops and restaurants are just within walking distance from this hotel.

Via Panizza 5 Centro, 20144

Phone: +39 02 469 0604

11 OTHER INTERESTING PLACES TO VISIT

All the colours of the market. Photo by Mike and Annabel Beales

Casa del Bianco

A traditional shop that sells classy household and bed linens, wonderful children clothes and shoes in original Italian style. This is place is definitely worth a visit.

Pellini

A famous Italian business in jewelry design now in its third generation. Designer Donatella Pellini uses materials such as glass, crystal and resin in its own original way. Marvel at the exquisite and elegant collections which are rare and limited.

Teatro Litta and Boccascena Cafe

Teatro Litta is Milan's most antique theatre with an impressive Lombard baroque architecture, which alone is worth a visit. Apart from Theatre performances there are also workshops and courses and there is a special program with performances for kids. Part of the Theatre is Boccascena Cafè a lunch and aperitive bar with an artistic interior.

Shopping in Milan

These are two words deeply entwined together: Milano and fashion. What follows next will be appreciation and it can only be done through shopping! On via Montenapoleone, you can find the heart of fashion trends and the most luxurious streets in the world. The streets of via del Gesù, via S. Andrea, via Spiga, via Borgospesso, are where you will find shops of the most famous Italian and international fashion designers. Here, you can go crazy with the latest designs in branded, signature dresses, bags and shoes, jewelry and even furniture. If you don't want to spend astronomical amounts you can opt to stroll along the famous Corso Vittorio Emanuele, where you can find shops offering less expensive but equally impressive goods.

12 MILAN TRAVEL ESSENTIALS

Currency

The Euro is the Milan's official currency and is available in eight different coins and seven separate bills. The Italian Euro is typically issued and controlled by European bank. Printed notes are available in 5, 10, 50, 100, 200, and 500. The coins are available in denominations of 1, 2, 5, 10, 20, and 50 cents.

Banks

In Milan, banks are generally open from Monday to Friday, with opening hours from 8:30 am to 1.30 pm. Depending on the bank it will reopen around 2/2.30pm and operate for a another hour and a half in the afternoon. Currency exchange booths are located near the airport, train stations as well as near the cathedral of Milan. ATMs can be found in the Milan's cathedral area, at train stations and airports. While most businesses in Milan accept bank debit cards and credit cards, it's still advisable to keep some cash on hand –especially for the markets.

Phone calls

Whether you want to call personal or business contact in Milan, there is a process that you will need to follow.

When calling Milan from the United States or Canada, you will be required to start with the exit code **011** followed by the country code **39** and then the city code **02** before finally keying in the local number. When calling Milan from Europe/globally begin with **00** and then country code + city code+ local number.

To dial a mobile phone from the United States or Canada, dial **011** followed by the country code **39** and then the **mobile number** *(varies by carrier but begins with a "3")* before finally keying in the local number. When calling from Europe/globally begin with **00** and then country code + mobile number.

If you are *in* Milan attempting to call someone outside Italy, then you need to dial the Italian international prefix (**00**), the code of the country you are calling, the area code and then the local number you are calling. For example, to call the United States from Milan you will start with the international prefix **00** followed by the country code **1** and then the area code **212** before finally keying in the local number.

To dial a local number *within* Milan, first dial the area code (**02**) followed by the local number.

Emergency number in Italy: Dial **113**

Business hours

Milan business hours are from 8.00 am to 1:00 pm and from 3:00pm to 7:00pm, Monday to Friday. Shops in Milan are usually open from 9:00 am to 7:30pm – Monday to Saturday. Big stores usually remain open during lunchtime and stay open later. Banks are closed on weekends and on holidays. The larger supermarkets will be open from Monday through Sunday while small shops operate Monday through Saturday, only.

During the weekdays, pharmacies are open from 8:00am to 7:30pm with a break between 1pm-4pm. A good tip to know is that most local pharmacies do not close at the same time. If you arrive at a pharmacy and it is closed, there will be a sign posted advising of the nearest location of a pharmacy that is open. Saturday hours are typically from 9:00am-1:00pm with closure on Sundays.

13 ITALIAN LANGUAGE ESSENTIALS

Italian is spoken by around sixty two million people globally and is the official language of Italy and one of the four national languages of Switzerland. Most travelers find it easy to pick up basic Italian because much of the vocabulary is similar to its English counterpart, such as museo (museum), studente (student), generale (general), parco (park), banca (bank) and so forth. Below, you will find a few common Italian phrases which you can use in everyday situations during your travels!

Greetings

Hello! – Salve! (*sAH-lveh*)

Good morning! – Buon giorno! (*bwon zhor-no)*

Good night – Buona notte! *(bwoh-nah noht-the)*

Hi! – Ciao! *(chow)*

Good Evening! Buona sera! (*bwoh-nah seh-rah)*

How are you? – Come sta? (*koh-meh STA?)*

Do you speak Italian? - Parla italiano? (*par-lah ee-tahl-ee-ah-no*)

What is the matter? - Cosa c'è? (*koh-zah cheh*)

Thank you very much – Grazie millie (*graht-zee-eh mee-leh*)

What is your name? – Come si chiama? (*KOH-meh see kee-AH-mah?*)

Where are you from? – Di dov'e sei? *(dee doh-veh seh-ee)*

OK! – Va bene! *(vah beh-neh)*

Directions

Where? – Dove? (*Doh-VEH*)

Where is the bus? – Dov'e l'autobus? *(doh-VEH low-TOH-boos)*

Where is the train? - Dov'e il treno? (*DOH-veh eel TREH-no*)

How do I get to _____ Come si arriva a_____ (*Koh-meh see ahr-REE-vah ah...?*)

Hotel –albergo (ahl-BER-go)

Restaurants – ristoranti *(rees-toh-RAHN-tee)*

Straight ahead – diritto (*dee-REET-toh*)

Street – strada (*STRAH-dah*)

Turn left – Si gira a sinistra (*EE-ree ah see-NEES-trah*)

Turn right – Si gira a destra (*EE-ree ah DEHS-trah*)

Past the – dopo il (*DOH-poh eel*)

Before the –prima del *(PREE-mah dehl)*

North – nord (*nohrd*)

South – sud (*sood*)

East -est (*ehst*)

West ovest (*OH-vehst*)

Please take me to____. Per favore, mi porti a _____ (*pehr fah-VOH-reh, mee POHR-tee ah*)

Stop here, please! – Ferma qui, per favore! (*FEHR-mah kwee pehr fah-VOH-reh*)

I'm in a hurry! – Vado di fretta! (*VAH-doh dee FREHT-tah*)

At the restaurant

I'm a vegetarian – Sono vegetariano/a (*SOH-noh veh-jeh-tah-RYAH-noh/ ah*)

I don't eat beef. – Non mangio il manzo. (*nohn

MAHN-joh eel MAHN-dzoh)

I don't eat pork. – Non mangio il maiale. (*nohn MAHN-joh eel mah-YAH-leh*)

Lunch – il pranzo (*eel PRAHN-dzoh*)

Chicken – il pollo (*eel POHL-loh*)

Fish – il pesce (*eel PEH-sheh*)

Beef– il manzo (*eel MAHN-dzoh*)

Sausage – salsiccia (*sahl-SEET-chah*)

Salad– insalata (*een-sah-LAH-tah*)

Eggs – uova (*WOH-vah*)

Cheese– formaggio (*fohr-MAHD-joh*)

The juice – il succo (*eel SOOK-koh*)

The beer – la birra (*lah beer-RAH*)

Excuse me, waiter? – Scusi, cameriere? (*SKOO-zee, kah-meh-RYEH-reh?*)

Please clear the table. Potete pulire il tavolo, per favore ((*poh-TEH-teh poo-LEE-reh eel tah-VOH-loh, pehr fah-VOH-reh*)

It was delicious. È squisito (*EH skwee-ZEE-toh*)

I'm done. Ho finito (*oh fee-NEE-toh*)

One more, please. Un altro, per favore (*oon AHL-troh, pehr fah-VOH-reh*)

Shopping

Expensive– caro (*KAH-roh*)

I am looking for something cheaper. Cerco qualcosa di più economico (*CHEHR-koh KWAHL-koh-zah dee pyoo eh-koh-NOH-mee-koh*)

OK, I'll take it. Va bene, lo prendo. (*vah BEH-neh, loh PREHN-doh*)

Want to take your Italian a step further?

The internet provides a great opportunity to get to know the Italian language. There are several free sites that can help you navigate your way through some simple phrases and allow you to listen to how Italian is spoken. Try www.oneworlditaliano.com. The BBC also offers a great online Italian course for free with helpful phrases, the Italian alphabet and links to Italian classes and courses. You can find it at http://www.bbc.co.uk/languages/italian/.

14 MILAN TOP THINGS TO DO

The Last Supper. The Last Supper by Leonardo Da Vinci is without doubt one of the best attractions in Milan which means tickets are in high demand. Booking in advance is a **must** and can be done through the official ticket site: http://www.vivaticket.it

The Milan Cathedral. The Duomo is the most iconic buildings housed within the center of Milan. To enjoy a breathtaking view from the cathedral, head to the roof. Thankfully, you can take advantage of the lift or more adventurous visitors can hike up the 150 steps. http://www.duomomilano.it/en/

Teatro Alla Scala. This is one of the famous opera houses in the world, featuring gold-plated and red velvet balconies. Tickets to opera performances are not as difficult to get as one would think. http://www.teatroallascala.org/en/

Villa Necchi Campiglio. The stunning Villa Necchi Campiglio is a place where great taste, glamour and good manners are given the top priority. Take a tour and discover more about this enthralling villa. http://www.visitfai.it/villanecchi/

Historic Art. Milan is one of Italy's cities that houses a wide range of art and galleries. One of the most famous being The Last Supper painted by Leonardo Da Vinci.

Consider Modern collections as well. You may be also interested in the modern artworks of Milan. There are several 20 century museums that can be visited throughout your stay.

Shop in style. Milan is a shopping mecca famous for selling clothes and other fashionable items. You will find a number of shopping malls and markets to suit your tastes, or those of friends back home.

10 Coso Como. The site was officially launched in 1990 as a fashion center. For those who are into fashion industry, you can greatly benefit from visiting this place. Prices are higher here however with a little hunting, you may find a few affordable items. http://www.10corsocomo.com/

Sant'Ambrogio. While many visitors often overlook Santa'Ambrogio in favor of Milan's Cathedral, the church is one of the Milan's most important historic buildings. Don't miss the golden alter and bronze casket located inside the cathedral. http://www.basilicasantambrogio.it/

Da Luigi. Enjoy a leisurely afternoon lunch with

friends at Luigi. Good company and a good glass of wine. This locale is one of the Milan's popular havens. http://www.daluigi.it

The Golden Rectangle (*Quadrilatero d'Oro*). The Golden Rectangle is characterized by fashion brands such as Dolce & Gabbana, Armani and other top fashion designers.

The Navigli Waterways. The Navigli is a network of canals that Leonardo Da Vinci played a critical role in developing.

Studio Achille Castiglioni. The studio was once owned by Achille, a famous furniture and industrial designer in Milan. Shelves are filled with secret drawers, inventions and models. http://www.achillecastiglioni.it/

Salone del mobile. Salone del mobile is the largest furniture show in Milan. It attracts more approximately 400,000 visitors across the world. http://salonemilano.it/en-us/

San Siro Stadium. The stadium was first constructed in 1925 and modified in 1990 for the world cup. It is a home for two main football clubs in Italy – Inter-Milan and AC Milan. http://www.sansiro.net/?lang=en

Unicredit Building. It is the tallest building in Milan that symbolizes the progress and pride of the city.

The Bull's Balls. Within the tiled floor of a building exists an artificial Bull and people spin on the Bull's balls. Why? It is believed that spinning on the Bull's balls can result in good luck for the person doing the spinning. In need of some good luck? It's located on the tiled floor of Galleria Vittorio Emanuele II.

Pinacoteca di Brera. This is one of Milan's finest museums. Here you will also find beautiful shops and leisure activities to enjoy.
http://www.brera.beniculturali.it/

Milan's parks. You can escape the bustle of Milan within its serene parks throughout the city center.

CONCLUSION

Milan is a quiet gem, a place which was able to carve its own niche as the most important financial city in Italy. It has many facets of interesting appeal as the city is a lifestyle destination offering a paradise for shopping, football, opera, and nightlife. All these attractions are served in a city with more than 26 centuries of rich history and remarkable heritage.

The city's innate charm may not captivate you at first glance. Rather, it may just look like an ordinary bustling and relatively stylish urban place. Unlike most European cities where the sights are visible upon arrival, you might need to spend more time exploring, strolling through unknown areas, to discover the beauty of Milan. Only then can you appreciate a diverse city, filled in every corner with history.

Here you will find a blend of cultural and historical influences from the various conquerors the past, all evident in the varying structures throughout the city. Perhaps, it is the diverse legacies that have made their mark which accounts for Milan's indescribable allure. A Milan experience is something that one may treasure for a long, long time. The thrill of discovery, and of learning, is something that can be acquired if one will just look deeper and go beyond the surface.

MORE FROM THIS AUTHOR

Below you'll find some of our other books that are popular on Amazon and Kindle as well. Alternatively, you can visit our author page on Amazon to see other work done by us.

3 Day Guide to Berlin: A 72-hour definitive guide on what to see, eat and enjoy in Berlin, Germany

3 Day Guide to Vienna: A 72-hour definitive guide on what to see, eat and enjoy in Vienna Austria

3 Day Guide to Santorini: A 72-hour definitive guide on what to see, eat and enjoy in Santorini Greece

3 Day Guide to Provence: A 72-hour definitive guide on what to see, eat and enjoy in Provence, France

3 Day Guide to Istanbul: A 72-hour definitive guide on what to see, eat and enjoy in Istanbul, Turkey

3 Day Guide to Budapest: A 72-hour Definitive Guide on What to See, Eat and Enjoy in Budapest, Hungary

3 Day Guide to Venice: A 72-hour Definitive Guide on What to See, Eat and Enjoy in Venice, Italy

Printed in Great Britain
by Amazon

24594914R00050